Gizmo

Michaela Morgan
Illustrated by Glen McBeth

Contents

OXFORD
UNIVERSITY PRESS

Mo's Mouse

My name is Mo Ghizi but everyone calls me:

GIZMO.

I'll tell you why.

First you have to meet my family.

Dad, the Professor (*brilliant*)

Mum (*brainy*)

Granny (*genius*)

Sister (*scientific*)

Me

Dog (*smelly*)

Baby Brother (*boffin*)

The Ghizi family are famous for making all sorts of inventions and gadgets and gizmos and I am determined to follow in their famous footsteps.

I've got a fantastic collection of all sorts of spare parts.

Look!

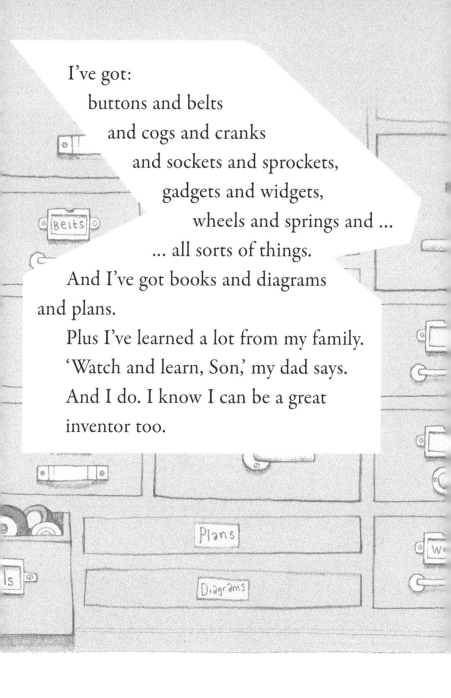

I've got:
  buttons and belts
    and cogs and cranks
      and sockets and sprockets,
        gadgets and widgets,
          wheels and springs and ...
      ... all sorts of things.
And I've got books and diagrams
and plans.
  Plus I've learned a lot from my family.
  'Watch and learn, Son,' my dad says.
  And I do. I know I can be a great
  inventor too.

I decided to start small ... and what is smaller than a mouse?

My gran is always saying things are as small as a mouse or as quiet as a mouse. I thought to myself, *small and quiet, what can go wrong?*

I decided to start with an old, broken thrown-away computer mouse and make it into a ...

ROBO MOUSE.

I rescued it from the bin and I gave it a make-over.

Changing its look was easy. I added ears, whiskers, two bright eyes, a tail and a cheeky smile.

I call it Click the mouse.

Of course there's more to a Robo Mouse than just its looks. It still had most of its wires and workings inside. So, with the help of a few plans and diagrams, books, a lot of thinking, a bit of help and some of my useful spare parts, I invented a mouse that could run forwards, zoom backwards and spin round and round. It could scuttle, squeak and leap – better than a real mouse.

It had three speeds:

Fast.

Super Fast.

And *Really Super Fast.*

9

However, I did get carried away. I decided it needed a remote control. I didn't have a spare one so I adapted the TV remote control.

We are all so busy inventing things at our house that we don't watch much TV, so it wasn't a problem at all ...

... until the day the babysitter came.

I don't really like having a babysitter.
Well, I'm not a *baby*, am I?

This babysitter is no fun at all. She never lets me do anything I want to do. No matter what I suggest, she always says:

She really is no fun at all.

All she ever wants to do is get the baby to bed, tell me to be quiet, tidy up and then slump in front of the telly shouting:

Don't make a mess!
Don't make a noise!

It was quiet. Mum and Dad were out. The baby was asleep. I was in my room, making no noise, making no mess. I was reading a book. I was as quiet as a mouse.

Then the babysitter started zapping through the channels.

She zapped backwards and forwards, pressing every button on the remote, trying to find something interesting to watch.

At first all she heard was a teeny tiny squeak.

Squeak.

Then something scuttled along the floor.

The babysitter *shrieked*.

This woke the baby ... who started howling.

Then Click the mouse zoomed round the room. It stopped right in front of the babysitter, went into a spin and JUMPED.

The babysitter leapt onto the table
and the table collapsed.

Food flew EVERYWHERE. There was
spaghetti and tomato sauce, roly-poly and
custard, and more. Much more!

The babysitter fell to the floor and tried
to run. She slid on some custard,
       slammed into the bookcase,
          which fell into the toys,
             which crashed into the plant pots,

                which smashed and splattered
                   the room with soil and petals.

In a way it was glorious. It was certainly
colourful. And noisy.

In my room I was quietly enjoying my book. I heard a crash.

Noisy! I thought.

I put down my book and went downstairs to see what was going on.

Messy! I thought.

I helped the babysitter up. I helped get the spaghetti out of her hair and I caught the mouse. I did *everything* I could to help but when Mum and Dad came home, they decided it was MY fault and they said ...

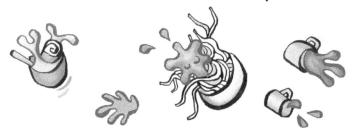

... well, I'd like to tell you exactly what they said but I don't think it was very polite.

The end result is that we need a new babysitter. And I've been given the job of clearing this mess up.

Mo's Machine

It's surprising how much mess one small, quiet mouse can make.

This will take me *weeks* to clean up.

Unless ...

I had a brilliant idea! I could make an automatic tidy-up machine.

I started work on my new machine.

It is AMAZING. I call it:

MO'S MAGNIFICENT TURBO TIDY.

It will:

- Tidy the books and toys.
- Walk the dog.
- Sweep the floor.
- Empty the bin.
- Mop the floor.

This time I did not make it remote controlled. It has a simple ON/OFF switch – and now is the time to turn it ON.

Countdown: 10, 9, 8, 7, 6, 5, 4, 3, 2, 1.
Go!
Isn't it brilliant?
Oh ...

    ... hmm.

Maybe one of the connections was wrong. My machine hesitated a bit, hissed once or twice and went BOING! Then it spluttered and went *bonkers*.

I tried to reach the OFF switch but with no luck.

On and on it went.
It tidied the bins.
It walked the toys.
It emptied the dog.
It mopped itself.

And it tried to sweep me.
Until ... finally ... it stopped.

Nothing I could do would get it going again.

So here I am sweeping and mopping, patting the dog and wishing that my baby brother was more help.

He has cleared up a bit of the food and one of the flowers, but really I wish I had a brother the same age as me. I'd like the sort of brother who would help me, someone I could play football with.

Hmm ... I'm getting another idea.

Mo's Match

I am a footy fanatic. I play for the school team and I'm the best goal scorer.

Actually I'm the *only* goal scorer.

My school is a village school. It's a very small village, so it's a very small school. And so our chances of winning any competitions against big schools are very small indeed. In fact they are teeny.

We only have two classes. One class is the big kids – but there aren't many of us. The other class is the little kids. Some of them are not much more than babies. So it's hard getting a football team of eleven together.

This is the team:

As you can see, we even have one of the infants playing for us.

He's small but he's nippy.

He's got a good, strong kick. He can kick the ball a *long* way.

Usually it's the *wrong* way but at least he can kick without falling over – which is a lot better than most of the other infants.

I practise my skills at home. I play against the garden wall and in every match with the garden wall, I win.

I work hard at practising my penalties but I think it would be a better match if there was a goalkeeper, so what do you think I did?

Yes.

With the help of some books, a diagram, a lot of thought, a bit of time and nearly all my spare parts, I made a robot to play football with me.

I call it ...
KICKBOT.

I let it wear my old kit and I have a kick about with Kickbot every evening.

As I add more to it, it looks better and better.

Of course, I have learned my lesson now. It is not remote controlled and it does not have a simple ON/OFF switch.

It is *voice activated.*

Oh yes! This is a bang-up-to-date, state-of-the-art, super-duper, voice activated Kickbot.

I tell Kickbot what to do and it does it.

'Kick!' I say, and it kicks.

'Catch!' I say, and it catches.

'Head the ball,' I command. Kickbot heads the ball.

'Dive!' I say
and he takes a dive.

This is my best robot yet!

Every day I teach Kickbot more tricks.

I decided Kickbot could be my lucky football mascot. So on the day of the big match ...

... I took him to school.

We were all very excited about the match. It was little old us versus the big new academy. *They* have loads of kids to make up a team. *They* have their own footy field, too.

We have to use the playground for our matches – and the infants get in the way sometimes with their sandpit and little tricycles.

The academy kids have a proper coach and they have a great kit. What they don't have is good sportsmanship. In fact, they are horrible to us every time we meet them. They cheat!

In past matches they have tried to distract the ref.

Once they hid his whistle ...

... and once they tied all our bootlaces together!

They know I'm a good goal scorer. I heard their captain talking about it. I couldn't hear exactly what they were saying but I know they were whispering and pointing at me.

Our team was ready. We'd made a great effort to make sure we all had some sort of kit and I had put in days of extra practice with Kickbot.

Plus we had a spare whistle for the ref – just in case.

We stood up straight, held our heads high, proudly ran onto the pitch, then ...

... Ouch!

Their captain tripped me up.

I *really* hurt my knee.

And I was out of the match.

Things were looking desperate. The game hadn't even started and we were already one player down.

We already had all the big kids in the team. Who could take my place?

The head teacher said, 'Not me!'

The lollipop lady said, 'Not me!'

The infants just said, 'Waaaaa!'

There was no one to replace me ...

... except Kickbot.

Kickbot followed my instructions.

'Run onto the pitch!'
He ran.
'Stand still!'
He stood still.
'Kick!'
He kicked.

In fact, he was brilliant. He took
control of the game, running here,
passing there, and scored a great goal.
We were 1–0 up!

It was all going well until ...

... Kickbot started to listen to the shouts
from the rest of the crowd.

> **Find a space!**

He ran off to find a space by himself.

> **Corner!**

He stood in the corner.
Then everyone started
shouting at the same time.

'Play it forward!'
shouted someone's dad.

'Careful at the back!'
said a teacher.

'Work hard, Academy, you'll score!'
said the academy's coach.

Kickbot stopped for a
second and his head turned
right round twice. He looked
up and down the pitch,
repeating, 'Forward,
back, score.'

Then he scored
another great goal.

He ran through a crowd of defenders, around the goalkeeper and shot.

No one could stop him.

The only trouble was ... he scored in *our* goal.

He had forgotten which way he was playing! I shouted for him to stop, but all he said was, 'Forward, back, score.' All the time his head kept spinning, looking from one goal to the other.

He kept scoring.

First at one end.

Then the other.

He was *unstoppable*.

I wish I could have stopped him.

It was all going badly.

And then it got worse.

It started to rain.

Kickbot ran slower and slower. I don't think the rain was good for him. He was rusting bit by bit, getting slower and slower and s l o w e r until he stopped.

He stopped just outside their penalty area and he wouldn't move an inch. There were only ten minutes of the game left and the score was 6–6. Kickbot had scored them all.

Bravely, my team played on, but it was hopeless. There was no way we could win now.

The team did its best. They didn't give up. Even the infant played on and on through the rain and mud. Finally, he gave the ball an almighty kick. It was going miles to the left of their goal of course, but ...

... it hit Kickbot's head.

Boing!

It bounced off Kickbot's head, over their goalkeeper and into the back of the net.

A perfect header! The winning goal.

YESSSSSSSS!

I took Kickbot home and gave him some extra oil but he was never quite the same. He still obeyed every command.

So I'm thinking it's about time I invented something new.

Now ... what should I make next? Have *you* got any ideas?

About the author

I am not much good at inventing robots and machines, but I am very good at making up stories. Ideas come from everywhere – from daydreams, other books, things I notice or overhear. I get some ideas from the many children I meet when I go to schools for Book Week.

I bet you could imagine a fantastic machine – and draw it. What about a machine to do your homework or a machine to find lost socks ... ?